NEW
3 -

A COURSE IN MARIGOLDS

FOUNDATION FOR DINNER PEAS

What others are saying about *A Course in Marigolds*

'A Course in Marigolds' is a delightful book that humorously applies the major principles of 'A Course in Miracles' to the world of inner gardening. If you have already undertaken the major Course, you will find this junior companion a refreshing and uplifting gift... This divinely zany little course will serve as a manual not just for growing, but for flying.

Alan Cohen, author, *The Dragon Doesn't Live Here Anymore*
From a review written for *New Realities Magazine*

We love it! It is such a clever idea and so well done! Your book has sprouted many seeds of laughter and joy.

Beverly Hutchinson
President, Miracle Distribution Center
Co-creator of the Miracle spoken tape/music series

"Sinless snails are my guide to peas.
Sinful snails are my guide to slime.
And which I choose to see
A Course in Marigolds showeth me."

Hugh and Gayle Prather
authors of *A Book for Couples*

Wonderful, marvelous, precious, good! I have read the entire course and I am thoroughly confused!

Jan Price
Co-founder, Quartus Foundation

The witty and purposeful humor of 'A Course in Marigolds' opens the reader's heart to concepts that the mind might otherwise resist. Reading it is not just planting seeds. It's walking into a fully flowering garden filled with delightful insights and colorful images.

Arnold Patent
Seminar leader and author, *Death Taxes & Other Illusions*

Thank you for an excellent parody of the books I treasure most.

Bob Burnett
Student of *A Course in Miracles*

The most hilarious take-off of 'A Course in Miracles' to date. Brace yourself, gentle reader, for 'A Course in Marigolds.' A hysterical collection of CIM-like text, lessons, and meditations. All those little 'ego-thoughts' you have been so ruthlessly repressing find voice here.

At first sight, we got so excited over this hilarious little volume that, as soon as we got up from the floor and could speak without giggling again, we called up to order a bunch. This little book truly is a young classic.

Kellie R. Love
Narrator of the audio version of *A Course in Miracles*
Editor of *Triangle Miracles Extension*

You did it! The book is a brilliant execution of parody. We laughed so hard tears rolled down our cheeks!

Paul & Layne Cutright
Relationship Educators

I am more than a little excited about your outstanding publication. It has been a real chuckle to casually give 'Marigolds' to friends and have them come to my office hours later with their faces beaming with a knowing kind of laughter, asking me without exception how to get more copies.

Christian Eddleman
Management Consultant

I love your book, and have been spreading it around. Keep up the gardening!

Marianne Williamson
Teacher and Lecturer of ACIM

A COURSE IN MARIGOLDS

COMBINED VOLUME

I
TEXT

II
WORKBOOK FOR STUDENT GARDENERS

III
MANUAL FOR GROWERS

FOUNDATION FOR DINNER PEAS

Revised Edition – Version 3.0

written by Michael Stillwater

This book is a parody of *A Course in Miracles*, a self-study program for shifting our perception from fear to love, and which may be obtained through the publisher, the Foundation for Inner Peace, Box 635, Tiburon, CA 94920.

Special thanks to the Foundation for Inner Peace for their willingess to laugh, to Kenneth Wapnick for his quote on the back cover, to all who contributed quotes to the forward section, and to the countless "marigold workers" who tirelessly and joyfully spread this little book around the world.

Published by
Inner Harmony Press
PO Box 450
Kula, HI 96790
U.S.A.

A COURSE IN MARIGOLDS

First Printing- October, 1988
Second Printing- November, 1988
Third Printing- February, 1989

ISBN 0-923860-00-2
Library of Congress Catalog Card Number pending
Manufactured in the United States of America

You are entitled to marigolds.

Workbook, Lesson 21

How It Came To Be

A COURSE IN MARIGOLDS began with the sudden decision of two people to join in an afternoon gardening project. Their names are unimportant. They were anything but gardeners. They had a history of trying to plant a garden, but continuously failing. The one who wrote down the material was the son of a Kansas farmer, and described himself:

"I always tried to grow plants- any kind at all- but never with any luck. They seemed to turn a cold shoulder to me. I had just about given up the idea of ever growing anything. And then something happened that triggered a chain of events I could never have predicted...my nextdoor neighbor unexpectedly announced that she wanted me to join her for an afternoon in her garden. As if on cue I agreed to help her out. Apparently this Course was to help *me* out."

Although their intention was serious, they found themselves kidding around a whole lot. But they had ventured close enough to the Plant Kingdom for It to use them for It's Purpose.

To continue the first-person account:

"Three uneventful hours preceded the actual writing, during which time we sprayed each other with the hose. Imagine how surprised I was when I heard a voice, 'This is a course in marigolds...' That was my introduction to the voice. It made no sound, but seemed to emenate from the nearby shrubbery. It seemed to be a special assignment I had somehow, somewhere agreed to complete. I still can't figure it out."

What It Is

As its title implies, the Course is arranged throughout as a teaching device. It consists of three booklets: a Text, Workbook for Gardeners, and Manual for Growers. The curriculum is quite absurd, leading an innocent reader into a confused world of warring snails. Nonetheless, the fact that the work is channeled from the Other Side must be evidence enough that there is something important here, important enough to consider long and hard. There are many other courses, but this is the only one which will relieve you of the notion that you are a good gardener, and replace it with a strong suspicion that you might be better off in the funny farm. What possible use is such a course? What is the reason for it's existence? Why did these inept gardeners go to the garden that fateful day? The answer to these, and many other questions, is what the *Course in Marigolds* is all about.

What It Says

"Nothing ventured, nothing gained,
nothing is left when nothing remains.
Herein lies the peace of gardeners."

This is how *A Course In Marigolds* begins. It makes a fundamental distinction between the gardener you secretly thought you were, and the truth about your inability to garden. This applies to everything you would try to grow- there are no exceptions.

A Course In Marigolds is quite consistent in what it presents, with the seeming goal of leading an incompetent gardener into a state of psychological torment by mentally fabricating a war of epic proportions with the snails. Why it wants to do this is unclear.

Some believe it to be a new dispensation, a way of coming into harmony with the plant kingdom. Others are convinced that it is all in code, a layered metaphysical text with deep submeanings. Many of these believers have formed study groups throughout the country, painstakingly comparing line-by-line the principles outlined in *A Course in Marigolds* with those taught in *A Course in Miracles*, a spiritual text remarkably similar in format, in a desperate attempt to unlock the secrets hidden within this sparse document. Still some, more skeptical readers, offer with wry speculation that it is actually channeled from an 18th century English gardener with a very twisted sense of humor.

Whatever you may believe, there is very little to go on. All that was dictated is the introduction, fifty principles, a brief and confusing chapter of text, twenty-four lessons, and the short introduction to a growers manual*, carefully salvaged from the original napkins and seed-packets which the scribe wrote it on. Thus the mystery stands unsolved. Who is it for? What is it's true purpose for mankind, and all garden varieties? Will we ever know? Will we ever really care? Why is anyone interested?

* Editors note: Since the publishing of the first edition of *A Course in Marigolds*, additional material has surfaced, all of which is included in this revised edition, version 3.0. The new material includes Text pages 22–25, Workbook page 49, and Manual pages 55-59, plus an Afterword describing the rapid proliferation of Marigold consciousness.

CONTENTS

TEXT

WORKBOOK FOR STUDENT GARDENERS

MANUAL FOR GROWERS

A COURSE IN MARIGOLDS

TEXT

FOUNDATION FOR DINNER PEAS

INTRODUCTION

This is a course in marigolds. It is a required course. Only the planting time is voluntary. Free will does not mean that you can establish the growing seasons. It means only that you can elect what you want to grow at a given time. The course does not aim at teaching the meaning of plants, for that is beyond what can be taught. It does aim, however, at removing the ignorance blocking the awareness of marigolds, which are your natural companions. The opposite of roots is fruits, but what is all over the plant are bugs.

This course can therefore be summed up very simply in this way:

Nothing ventured, nothing gained.
Nothing is left when nothing remains.

Herein lies the peace of gardeners.

Chapter 1

THE MEANING OF MARIGOLDS

Principles of Marigolds

1. There is no order of beauty in marigolds. One is not "prettier" or "more gorgeous" than another. They are all the same. All expressions of gardening are nice, and if sold, taxable.

2. Marigolds as such do not matter. The only thing that matters is their fertilizer, which is far beyond compost.

3. Marigolds occur naturally in the wild. The real marigold is always inspiring. In this sense everything that grows is inspiring.

4. All marigolds are alive, and watering helps. Your Guidebook will direct you very specifically. You will be told all you need to know.

5. Marigold growing is a habit, which should be involuntary. It should not be consciously planned out, or you may discover you should never have gotten into gardening in the first place.

6. Marigolds are natural. If they are dying, something has gone wrong.

7. To grow marigolds is everyone's right, but fertilization is necessary first.

8. Marigolds are inedible yet still may supply a dietary lack; they are sometimes eaten by those who temporarily have less color in their salads, and served to those who are unaware of the ruse.

9. Marigolds can be exchanged. Like all expressions of gardening, which are always natural in the true sense, the transaction reverses the situation, whereby now you have money, but no marigolds.

10. The use of marigolds as spectacles to induce compliments from your neighbors and guests is a misunderstanding of their purpose.

11. Earth is the medium of marigolds. It is a means of transmitting the needed moisture and minerals to the plant. Through the earth, nutrients are received, and through the flower, pretty colors are expressed.

12. Marigolds have thoughts. They think about the lower, or dirty things, and also about higher, leafier things.

13. Marigolds have both beginnings and endings, so don't expect them to live forever.

14. Marigolds bear witness to their gardener. They are convincing when you've done a good job. Without conviction, they deteriorate into mulch, which gets quite muddy when it rains.

15. Each day should be devoted to marigolds. The purpose of time is to enable you to learn how to grow marigolds well. The marigolds will cease to flower when you are no longer a useful gardener.

16. Marigolds are teaching devices for demonstrating your competence or incompetence as a gardener. They simultaneously bolster your ego and look pretty.

17. Marigolds transcend the common weeds. They may suddenly shift their position in your garden when you aren't looking.

18. Growing marigolds is a service. It is the maximal service you can render to your garden. It is a way of giving fresh flowers to your neighbors. You recognize your own and your flower's worth simultaneously, as the neighbor trys to pay you for them.

19. Marigolds make you one with your garden. They depend on your cooperation because the Plant Kingdom loves to be fertilized, weeded, and watered. Marigolds therefore reflect the laws of good gardening, not of your "great gardening ideas".

20. Marigolds reawaken the awareness that gardening can be fun. This is the recognition that leads to the appealing power of the marigold.

21. Marigolds are natural signs of forgiveness. Through gifts of potted marigolds you let your neighbors and friends know how sorry you are to have forgotten them as you spend more and more hours in the garden.

22. Marigolds are associated with fear only because of the belief that flowers have eyes, and are watching you and conspiring against you.

23. Marigolds rearrange your priorities and place everything else in disorder. This can be disturbing to your family, as they may never see you again.

24. Marigolds enable you to attempt healing the sick, as you prepare strange herbal concoctions for your ailing neighbors.

25. Marigolds can be made into an interlocking chain of flowers, similar to a daisy chain, which when completed could stretch around the world- if you had that many flowers.

26. Marigolds represent freedom from fear. The fears you always had about just hanging out in the garden without any visible means of financial support simply fly away, as do your friends, social conscience, and bank account.

27. A marigold is a universal blessing from the gardener, through the local flower shop, to all the world. It is the privilege of the gardener to garden.

28. Marigolds are a way of earning a living, but only very rarely.

29. Marigolds praise God through you. This happens on those occasions when gardeners become trance-mediums for their flowers, and the marigolds begin singing songs and uttering strange sounds through them.

30. By recognizing your inadequacy as a gardener, marigolds adjust their own levels of water and fertilizer until they are properly aligned. This is done at night, when you are asleep.

31. Marigolds should inspire gratitude, not "awww- look at the cute flowers!" You should thank your lucky stars for having the chance to plant a garden. Old watering cans can be hidden, but never lost.

32. All marigold seeds should come from the central supply house, or they may be defective. This assures you of perfect marigolds, as long as you follow directions.

33. Marigolds honor you because you are lovable, in a funny kind of way. They dispel illusions about yourself, like "Boy, I am a good gardener- aren't I?", and perceive the truth in you, like "I don't know very much about gardening, do I?"

34. Marigolds restore the garden to its former greatness. By filling in the empty spaces, they establish a protective foliage around the perimeter. Together with blackberry bushes, they make slow going for intruders.

35. Marigolds are expressions of love, but they may not always look that way. (Keep trying).

36. Marigolds are examples of right thinking. You had a good idea, you planted marigolds, you gardened- the yard still doesn't look too great. (Keep it up).

37. A marigold can help to correct a poorly designed garden. It acts as a catalyst, breaking up erroneous weeds and insignificant plantings and reorganizing the yard properly. This places you under the "Proper Gardening" principle, where poor gardens are made good. Until this has occurred, a beautiful yard is impossible.

38. The Weed Eater is a great mechanism for helping grow marigolds. Just remember which are the flowers, and which are the weeds. Otherwise you're going to have a lot of marigolds flying around like crazy.

39. The marigold dissolves your marriage if you spend all your time in the garden, and don't go in the house anymore. This is the same as saying that by perceiving an empty closet, your spouse has probably already disappeared.

40. The marigold makes a nice gift to your brother or mine. It is a way of perceiving the universal mark of a good gardener. Only, why are you giving marigolds to my brother?

41. Wholesome sandwiches with a content of marigolds can make for a strange lunch, or a strange snack, for that matter.

42. A major contribution of marigolds is their strength in releasing you from your false sense of isolation, deprivation, and lack. Just look! You have a whole garden full of little friends, eager to please you.

43. Marigolds arise from a "marigold" state of mind, or a state of "marigold-readiness".

44. The marigold is an expression of an inner awareness of "I really want to grow something pretty," and the acceptance of this idea into your consciousness.

45. A marigold is never lost. It may touch many people you have not even met, and produced undreamed of changes in situations of which you are not even aware. For example, a neighbor might secretly take a few blossoms while you are away. Unknown to them, tiny spiders come along for the ride. Then, while giving these flowers to her boss, the tiny spiders run all over the floor, causing an uproar, and making for an interesting conversation piece around the office. Meanwhile, you weren't even aware of it.

46. Marigolds are only temporary— like office help.

47. The marigold is an economizing device that lessens the need for purchasing flowers at the supermarket. It establishes an out-of-pocket expense not deductible under the usual laws of the state. In this sense it is not really economical.

48. The marigold is a plant that, if it dies and begins to smell, you want to immediately dispose of it.

49. The marigold makes no distinction among degrees. You can have a B.A., and M.A., or even a PhD in Horticulture- the marigold doesn't care. This is its true indiscriminateness.

50. The marigold compares what you have done with how good a real gardener can do, and hopefully you will not fail in the comparison.

Elevation, Lime, and Marigolds

Elevation induces complete but temporary suspension of a sense of stability. It reflects the original form of vertigo, if you go up too high. This is why it is best to plant your garden close to the ground. Physical closeness to other gardeners is nice, but you cannot achieve optimum motion with your trowel and hoe if you are too close to someone else. Marigolds, however, are genuinely interpersonal, and their planting results in true closeness to others. Proper elevation unites you directly with the earth. Marigolds unite you directly with your brother, if he happens to be working on the garden with you. A consciousness of boredom is the state that induces you to garden, though it does not inspire it. You are free to believe what you choose, and what you do better be good.

Gardening is intensely personal and cannot be meaningfully translated into Eskimo, due to the cold arctic climate. That is why any attempt to describe it in words is impossible. Gardening induces lots of experience. Marigolds, on the other hand, induce action. They are useful to you now because of their interpersonal nature. In this phase of learning, planting marigolds is important because freedom from fear about your inability as a gardener cannot be thrust on you. True gardening is being literally unspeakably dirty, because it is an experience of unspeakable filth.

"Awww" should be reserved for when you see little baby animals, to which it is perfectly and correctly applicable. It is not appropriate for marigolds because a state of "Awww" is sickeningly sweet, implying that you have forgotten you are gardening for a deep inner purpose. The marigold is therefore a sign of good gardening practice between equals. Equals should not be going "Awww" to one another's flowers because "Awww" implies you are getting much too sentimental.

The marigold minimizes the need for lime in your fertilizer, and may cause other interesting situations. In the longitudinal or horizontal plantbeds the recognition of the different growing flowers and vegetables appears to involve an endless making of little signs. However, the marigold occasionally will suddenly shift vertically, introducing itself to you on a firstname basis, which may cause you to step in out of the sun for a short period. The marigold thus has the unique property of abolishing your plans for a quiet afternoon of gardening to the extent that it renders the interval of time spent in the shade unproductive. There is no relationship between the time a marigold takes from you and the time it takes to recover. The marigold will try to substitute "shortcut gardening tips" for garden learning that might have taken thousands of hours, but don't listen to them. They are only playing on your sense of fatigue, your highly vulnerable imagination, and it is best to rest before you collapse in time.

Distortions of Marigolds

Your distorted approaches to gardening produce a dense cover of weeds over your marigolds, making it harder for them to reach the light of day. The confusion of marigolds with dandelions and poppies is a major perceptual distortion. These distortions often lead to misdirected labelling of your flowers, both in the garden and the mind. Remember that all real pleasure comes from gardening. This is because *not* doing it is a denial of your natural propensity for gardening. Denial of your natural propensities results in shabby gardens, while correct gardening procedures brings release from all embarrasment. Do not deceive yourself into thinking that you can ever again relate to your flowers or your bushes without this Course- you can't turn back now, my friend.

Son of Sod, you were created to plant beautiful gardens, design great landscapes, and devise ingenious fountainworks. Do not forget this. Every evening, the beauty of nature, for a little while, must still be only guessed at by you and your neighbors, because your outdoor lighting is still so dim. You can use your roto-tiller best to help you enlarge your landscaped area so you can achieve real satisfaction, of which you are incapable now. Learning to do this is the roto-tiller's only true usefulness.

Fantasy is fun, we know, but may lead to distorted forms of gardening. Fantasy tends to distract you, leading you to make imaginative yet unstylish arrangements by twisting little plant tendrils around each other. Gardening includes working with stems, leaves, and flowers, but you still don't know what you do, do you? Fantasy is an attempt to build a garden out of false seeds. You believe in what you grow. If you offer marigolds, you will be equally strong in your belief in them. Complete restoration of the garden is the only goal of the marigold-minded.

This is a course in garden training. All learning involves attention and study at some level, and it looks like we're going to have to begin at a very basic level with you. A solid foundation is necessary because of the tendency for gardens built on quicksand and in cesspool areas to dissolve into mush. It would be unwise to start on the more advanced aspects of this course, such as building gardens in quicksand, until you have mastered the basics, such as planting something in the soil that actually grows. If you try to rush things, your gardening may turn out to be a traumatic experience. The blossoms come of themselves in the end. The details are being carefully explained to you. Your developing green thumb may occasionally reveal some garden secrets, but to reach garden mastery the correct means are needed.

The Function of the Marigold Gardener

Before marigold gardeners are ready to undertake their function in the garden, it is essential thet they fully understand the fear of spiders, snails, and earthworms. Otherwise they may unwittingly foster the belief that there is nothing to worry about while gardening, a belief that is already very prevalent.

This interpretation arises in turn from the belief that these little guys can only get you if you have shorts on, which is because you believe they aren't smart enough to figure other ways of reaching you while you're not looking, even with long pants on.

A strong insect repellant is a far better protective device than any form of mental denial, such as repeating to yourself "there are no bugs, nothing's gonna get me", etc. To amplify an earlier statement, "the opposite of roots is fruits, but what is all over the plant are bugs." Thus the bugs are a part of the garden, whether you like it or not.

Marigolds are an expression of marigold-mindedness, and marigold-mindedness means marigold-readiness. The garden-minded are simple-minded, and the simple-minded are kind of slow. This is why gardeners work slowly, and gardens grow slowly.

The sole responsibility of the marigold-gardener is to answer the phone for himself. This means you recognize the ringing sound is not in your head, but coming out of the house. Furthermore, it means you must not expect your husband or wife, son or daughter, or itinerant roommate to answer the blasted phone for you. It's none of their business, and they probably wouldn't take the message down correctly anyway. Just because you happen to be a hundred yards away, huffing and puffing, with your hands completely covered in grime, why should you deserve special treatment? If the phone rings, answer it, or get yourself a machine.

Special Principles of Marigold Gardners

1. The marigold abolishes the need for lower-order concerns, such as taking phone messages. Since it is out-of-pattern for you to be gardening in the first place, the ordinary considerations of social behavior do not apply. When you plant a marigold, you are free to be as crazy as you like.

2. A clear distinction between what is planted and what is plastic, or artificial, is essential. All forms of garden awareness rest on this fundamental understanding- you have to tell the difference between an artifical plant and a real one.

3. Never confuse your left and right foot. Putting on the wrong shoe in the morning will make your day miserable, a painful and unnecessary experience, unless you really enjoy the pain.

4. The marigold doesn't care one way or the other. Being without concern, it just wonders how you could be so dumb as to mix up your shoes.

5. Try not to judge your flowers to harshly. They are doing the best they can. Give them time- they'll change.

6. You can do much on behalf of your own garden mastery and that of others if, in a situation which calls for your attention, you think of it this way:

I am here only to be a truly good gardener.
I am here to represent the local Garden Club.
I do not have to worry about what to say or what to do, because it's all written very clearly in the manual.
I am content to be here in the garden all day long, knowing the flowers need me.
I will be here, unless I am there.

Hose Once Again

Dehydration has one lesson it would teach, in all its forms, wherever it occurs in your flowerbeds. It would persuade you to consider investing in a sprinkler system, or irrigation of some kind. The plants are unable to escape the heat, whereas you can blithely go into the shade whenever you choose. Their immobility sets the limits on what they can do- their greatest hope is in your kindness, even your intelligence, to appreciate their peril. Would you still deny them their daily drink, if the flowers were to speak as one voice, asking you but this:

"Hose once again if you would take your place among the saviors of the garden, or observe us withering away into dried leaves before your unsympathetic eyes."

How could you not water after an experience like this? That is easily explained! You simply deny that you ever heard the flowers speaking to you, dismissing it as a silly figment, and return to your TV. Yet still you wonder– should I hose again? Learn, then, the happy habit of response to all dehydration within your garden, by repeating these words.

> *"I am willing to hose again because it has to be done. I am a channel for the water to flow to the flowers, and need not suffer feeling guilty anymore."*

What you behold as sick and weak flowers are but a reflection of your own thoughts about your gardening abilities, which are sick and weak thoughts. Yield not to this, and you will behold the sick flowers stand up and walk. A marigold has come to heal your mind, and close the toolshed door upon dreams of lousy gardening habits, opening the way to your eventual release from your present occupation as an account executive. Hose once again, remembering that every hosing brings you one step closer to total soil saturation, thus establishing your identity as a gardener, if you believe it is so.

Brother in plant care, do not fail to listen well to the advice presented here. We ask for nothing but peas, and some marigolds as well. Perhaps a row of corn, tomatos, cucumbers, and squash would be nice also. While you're at it, why not make that ten rows each, plus a plot of radishes, lettuce, and watermelon. To your tired eyes we bring a vision of a beautiful garden, so new and clean and fresh you wouldn't believe it possible without a tremendous expenditure of energy- and this is so.

Let us be glad that we can walk the garden, finding so many chances to be helpful. And thus will all vestiges of snails, secret rubbish piles and hidden weed patches be gone. And all the loveliness they concealed appear like heavenly lawns, until you roto-till them to plant marigolds anew.

And now we say, "Hey, Man!" This is only because we want to get your attention. For we have reached you where we know we can find you, in your home, until we convince you that you need to spend more time outside, in which case we will find you forever in your garden.

A COURSE IN MARIGOLDS

WORKBOOK
FOR
STUDENT GARDENERS

FOUNDATION FOR DINNER PEAS

INTRODUCTION

A theoretical foundation such as the text provides is necessary as a framework to make the exercises in this workbook meaningful. Yet it is doing the exercises that will make the goal of the course possible. An untrained gardener can accomplish nothing. It is the purpose of this workbook to train you until you have completely forgotten your lousy approach.

The exercises are very simple. They do not require a great deal of intelligence, and it does not matter where you do them. They need no preparation. The training period is many, many years. Do not undertake to plant more than one new garden per season (unless you think you're really something special).

Some of the ideas the workbook presents you will find hard to believe, and others may seem to be quite startling. A few may even give you a case of the heebee-geebies. This does not matter. You are merely asked to apply the ideas as you are directed to do. You are not asked to write the book. You are asked only to use these ideas. It is their use that will give them meaning to you, hopefully, and will show you that they are actually pretty good ideas, more or less.

Remember only this; you need not believe the ideas, you need not accept them, and you need not even welcome them. Some of them you may actively resist. None of this will matter, or decrease their efficacy. But do not allow yourself to make exceptions in applying the ideas the workbook contains- we have ways of finding out if you're trying to cut corners. And whatever your reactions to the ideas may be, use them. Nothing more than that is required. Got it?

LESSON 1

"Nothing I plant in this room
[on this table, in this garden, on this windowsill]
seems to grow anyway."

Now look slowly around you, and practice applying this idea very specifically to whatever you see:

"This tomato plant does not seem to grow."
"This begonia does not seem to grow."
"This cactus does not seem to grow."
"This bonsai garden does not seem to grow."

Then look farther away from your immediate area, and apply the idea to a wider range:

"That rose bush does not seem to grow."
"That apple tree does not seem to grow."
"That grapevine does not seem to grow."
"That oak tree does not seem to grow."
"That field of strawberries does not seem to grow."

Notice that these statements are not arranged in any order, and make no allowances for differences in the kinds of plants to which they are applied. That is the purpose of the exercise. The statement should merely be applied to any growing thing you see. As you practice the idea for the day, use it totally indiscriminately. Do not attempt to apply it to every single plant you see, for these exercises should not become ritualistic. Only be sure that no plant you see is specifically excluded. One plant is like another as far as the application of the idea is concerned.

Each of the first three lessons should not be done more than twice a day each, preferably morning and evening, sitting in your garden. Nor should they be attempted for more than a minute or so, unless that entails a sense of leisure. A harried, distraught pace is helpful.

LESSON 2

"I have given all the plants I see in this room [in this garden, on this windowsill, in this place] all the fertilizers I could possibly buy."

The exercises with this idea are similar to the previous one, except now we are talking about fertilizers. Begin with the plants that are near you, and apply the idea to whichever ones your glance rests on. Then increase the range outward. Turn your head so that you include whatever wilting flora is on either side. If possible, turn around and apply the idea to any plants that might be languishing behind you. Remain as indiscriminate as possible in selecting subjects for its application, do not concentrate on anything in particular, and do not attempt to include every growing thing you see in a given area, or you may introduce mental fatigue- now that would be silly, wouldn't it?

By examining your poor choice of fertilizers, and how you have been consistently unsuccessful in making the right choice, you will gradually be led to depend on this guide for all the right gardening choices.

LESSON 3

"I do not understand anything about gardening [in this place, in that place, inside or outside, or anywhere- I just don't understand]."

Apply this idea in the same way as the previous ones, without making distinctions of any kind between your zucchinis, ivy, or squash. Be sure that you do not question the suitability of this statement- or any other statement in this course. These are not exercises in judgment. Who do you think you are, trying to judge, anyway?

It is essential that you keep a perfectly open mind about these things. It is really for your own good that we are reminding you of this simple truth. Even the lawn can be seen with new eyes, as you recognize you haven't got what it takes- until now, using the daily lessons of A Course In Marigolds.

We are gradually leading you to a new awareness of your complete incompetence as a gardener. Only as you begin to recognize what an utter failure you have been, can you be open the new and revolutionary ideas which this course presents.

LESSON 4

"My thoughts about gardening don't mean anything."

Unlike the preceding ones, these exercises do not focus on your gardening itself. They focus, in contrast, upon your disturbing thoughts about gardening.

> Why can't I garden properly?
> Why can't I roll up the hose so it doesn't look like a big mess?
> Why can't my lawn be green instead of brown?
> Why can't my neighbors have uglier gardens?

Ask yourself these and similar disquieting questions throughout the day.

LESSON 5

"I am never upset by the snails- I think."

This idea can be used in any situation where you find yourself today. Imagine you are in your garden, seeing hordes of snails chewing upon the very vegetables and flowers which you toiled for months to grow. Is this upsetting you? Or are you pretending it's not upsetting, and pretending that what *really* upsets you is your job, your relationship, your finances, your aching back. Look more closely, and see if perhaps all these other "ailments" are merely disguising the real cause of your upset- the snails in your little garden.

When using the idea for today for a specific perceived cause of an upset in any form, use both the name of the form in which you see the upset, and the cause which you ascribe to it. For example:

> *"I am not angry at__________for the reason I think."*
> *"I am not afraid of__________for the reason I think."*

These statements reflect the newfound thought entering your consciousness- the question which emanates from deep within- could the real cause of your upset, after all, be...the snails?

It might help to precede the longer exercises with the statement:

> *"Snails may be small, but they sure upset me in a big way.*
> *They are all equally disturbing to my peace of mind."*

Then examine your mind for whatever is distressing you, regardless of how much or how little you think it is doing so. You may also find yourself less willing to apply today's idea to some perceived sources of upset than to others. If this occurs, think first of this:

> *"I cannot keep this form of upset and let the others go. It's either all the snails fault, or else I'm just wasting my time with these funny exercises."*

Repeat this idea at least three hundred and forty times today.

LESSON 6

"I am upset because I see snails everywhere."

The exercises with today's idea are very similar to the preceding ones, and are leading you into a new state of awareness, in which you will gradually begin seeing those viscous little snails everywhere. Apply this idea when in the bathroom, in the kitchen, in the office, and on the freeway. By thinking through with this idea constantly, you *will* begin to see snails everywhere.

Repeat this idea whenever you get bothered today:

> *"I am angry at____________because I see snails everywhere."*
> *"I am worried about____________because I see snails everywhere."*

Today's idea is useful for application to anything that seems to upset you, and can profitably be used throughout the day if you are able to sell the idea for cash to anyone who may be interested. However, the three or four practice periods which are required should be preceded by a minute or so of snail searching, as before, followed by an application of snail repellant to each upsetting mollusk uncovered in the search.

LESSON 7

"I see only the snails."

This idea is particularly difficult to believe at first. Yet it is the obvious outcome of the previous ideas.

It is the reason why nothing you plant seems to grow anyway.
It is the reason why your fertilizers have been ineffective.
It is the reason why you don't understand anything about gardening.
It is the reason why you're wife or husband wants to leave you.
It is the reason why you have been upset for all these years.
It is the reason why you are such a terrible gardener.

Old ideas about snails are very difficult to change, because everything you believe about them is rooted in the idea that they can't ruin your whole life. Yet that is precisely why you need new ideas about snails. This idea is not really so strange as it may sound at first.

Look at a cup, for example. Do you see a cup, or are you merely thinking that it is a cup, when actually it could be a large snail? Pick up the cup, and rub it against your face. What if you were really rubbing a large snail against your face? How would you feel? What would be different in your perception?

Look about you. This is equally true of whatever you look at. Acknowledge this by applying the idea for today indiscriminately to whatever catches your eye. For example:

> *"I see only the snails on this pencil."*
> *"I see only the snails on this shoe."*
> *"I see only the snails on this hand."*
> *"I see only the snails on that body."*
> *"I see only the snails on that face."*

Do not linger over any one thing in particular, but remember to omit nothing specifically. Glance briefly at each subject, long enough to see the snails, and move on to the next. Three or four practice periods, each to last an hour or so, will be enough.

LESSON 8

"My mind is preoccupied with snails."

This idea, is of course, the reason why you see only the snails. No one really sees anything but those crawly creatures if their mind is preoccupied with them long enough. The mind's preoccupation with snails is the cause of all your suffering.

The one wholly true thought one can hold about the snails is that they may not be there, but then again– maybe they are. To think about them at all is therefore to think about illusions. Very few have realized what is actually entailed in picturing the snails or in anticipating their return after dark. The mind is actually blank with terror when it does this, because it is not really thinking about anything happy.

The exercises for today should be done with eyes closed. (No peeking!) This is because you actually cannot see anything when your eyes are closed, and it is easier to recognize that no matter how vividly you may picture a thought about the snails, it is never as gross as when you open your eyes and see them crawling right in front of you. With as little investment as possible, search your mind for the usual minute or so, merely noting the snail images you find there. Name each one by a special name you assign to it, such as 'Mortimer', 'Bonnie', 'Ajax', 'Euclid', etc. Introduce the practice period by saying:

> *"I seem to be thinking about___________."*

Then name each of your thoughts specifically, for example:

> *"I seem to be thinking about [name of a person], about [name of an object], about [name of an emotion]."*

and so on, concluding at the end of the mind-boggling period with:

> *"But my mind is preoccupied with snails."*

This can be done forty or fifty times during the day, unless you find it irritates you. If you find it trying, try doing it a hundred times- that'll *really* irritate you.

LESSON 9

"I see nothing but snails now."

This idea obviously follows from the two preceding ones. But while you may be able to accept it intellectually, it is unlikely that it will mean anything to you as yet. However, understanding is not necessary at this point. In fact, the recognition that you do not understand is a prerequisite for undoing your false ideas. These exercises are concerned with practice, not with understanding. You do not need to practice what you already understand. It would indeed be quite stupid to aim at understanding, and assume that you have it already- huh? If you want understanding, go buy an encyclopedia.

You are getting closer with this idea to the complete denial of everything that was reality before, and opening to the new possibility of a life of total gardening.

LESSON 10

"The snails don't mean anything."

This idea reminds you that the snails don't mean anything– they don't mean to offend you by their rude acts of wanton, callous destruction. They don't mean to harm your sense of decency about what an animal *should* look like. In short, they don't mean anything by their obnoxious behavior.

Close your eyes for today's exercises, and introduce them by repeating the idea for today quite slowly to yourself. Then add:

> *"The snails don't mean anything when they leave a sticky trail in front of me."*
> *"The snails don't mean anything when they look at me with their skinny little eye-pods."*
> *"The snails don't mean anything when they gobble my garden."*

Remember to repeat the idea slowly before applying it specifically, and also add:

> *"This idea will help to release me from all that I now believe."*

LESSON 11

"My thoughts are meaning less and less all the time."

This is the first idea we have had for some time that is really helpful. It is an idea which will transform your way of seeing yourself. It will show you what a turkey you have been. It will show you that you really don't have any idea whatsoever about what this course is about, or what you are about, or what your garden is about. How about that?

LESSON 12

"I am upset because my thoughts are meaning less and less."

The importance of this idea lies in the fact that you still get upset over the fact that you can't garden worth a hoot, and your thoughts about everything of any value are going down the drain.

As you look about you, say to yourself:

> *"I think I see giant green spiders, monstrous centipedes, scary scorpions, and deadly bees."*

and so on, using whatever descriptive terms happen to occur to you. If terms which seem positive rather than negative occur to you, include them. For example, you might think of a "good green spider", or "a satiated python". At the end of the practice period, add:

> *"But I am upset because my thoughts are meaning less and less."*

Once is enough for practicing the idea for today. This should sufficiently confuse you to last for a long, long time.

LESSON 13

"I'm afraid that I'm going crazy."

Today's idea is really another form of the preceding one, except that it is more specific as to the emotion aroused. Actually, your thoughts have been meaning less and less for a long time now. This course is only helping you to see this, and accept the inevitable conclusion that you are, indeed, going bananas.

It is essential, therefore, that you prepare a padded room for yourself, a place to go when you can't garden anymore for fear of seeing the snails crawling about you.

The exercises for today, which should be done about three or four times a minute, include reaching for invisible bugs which are flying around your head all the time. This should be done with the eyes closed. Then open your eyes, look about you slowly, saying:

"I really am going crazy!"

Repeat this statement to yourself as you look about. Then close your eyes, and conclude with:

"How did I ever get into this course, anyway?"

You may find it difficult to avoid feeling sorry for yourself at this point, in one form or another. Whatever form this self-pity takes, remind yourself that you are really afraid of what the snails might do to you if they find you alone after dark, without a flashlight.

LESSON 14

"What I see in my garden is a form of vengeance."

Today's idea accurately describes the way anyone who has come this far with A Course In Marigolds will see their garden. The newly planted marigolds stand posed, about to strike you. Your rosebushes carefully yet silently aim their thorns at you. You see the snails quietly gathering to form a vigilante posse, just waiting for sundown to come after you.

This becomes an increasingly vicious picture until you are willing to change your approach to gardening. Otherwise, thoughts of counter-attack will preoccupy you. What peace of mind is possible to you then?

It is from this savage fantasy that you want to escape. Is it not joyous news to hear that the snails are putting off their attack until tomorrow evening? Is it not a happy discovery to find that you have escaped— until then? You made what you would destroy; now your garden, for which you have slaved all these months, is turning against you.

At the end of each practice period, ask yourself:

"Am I prepared to ward off tomorrow's snail attack?"

The answer is surely obvious.

LESSON 15

"I can escape from my garden hell by surrendering to the snails before sundown."

The idea for today contains the only way out of fear that will ever succeed. Nothing else will work; everything else is meaningless. But this way cannot fail. The garden you see is a vengeful garden, and everything in it is a symbol of vengeance. One can well ask if you are off your rocker. Is not fantasy a better word for such a process, and hallucination a more appropriate term for the result?

The idea for today introduces the thought that you are not trapped in your house, because you can negotiate a surrender. This surrender requires, first, that you identify yourself to the captain of the snails. Don't try any tricks, or this may be your last garden party!

In your practice periods, go over again and again what you are going to say to the captain of the snails when you surrender. Leave out no detail, however seemingly insignificant. It is vitally important to your survival that you act according to proper snail etiquette, which includes offering a gift of your favorite appetizer (unsalted, of course– and *never* offer escargot.)

LESSON 16

"The snails are attacking my defenses- am I invulnerable?"

It is surely obvious that if you can be attacked you are not invulnerable. You see this attack as a real threat. That is because you believe that snails can really attack you. And that would have a detrimental effect on your health, if they succeeded. They are disobeying the laws of man and nature, as well as common garden courtesy, and it is this law that will ultimately save you- but you are misusing it now. You must therefore learn how it can be used for your own best interests, rather than against them.

Because the snails smell your fear, you will fear attack. And if you fear attack, you must believe that you are not invulnerable. It is very important to build some battlements around your house, separating you from the garden, if you are to successfully fend off the invading mollusk hordes.

The practice period should begin with repeating the idea for today, then closing your eyes and reviewing the unresolved questions whose outcomes are causing you concern:

> *Could they be entering through the basement?*
> *Have they taken my dog or cat as prisoner?*
> *What is the best counter-attack?*
> *What could they possibly want from me?*

LESSON 17

"Above all else I want to see this thing work out OK."

Today we are developing a justifiable desire for a peace truce. In these practice periods, you will be making a series of definite commitments. The question of whether you will keep them in the future is not our concern here, as it is highly probable that you will retract any agreements you make with the snails as soon as your garden is safe again.

When you say "Above all else I want to see this thing work out OK," you are making a commitment to withdraw your preconceived ideas about the negotiations. You are not defining them in past terms. You are asking what is happening, rather than telling the snails what it is you want.

This willingness on your part is a very good idea, as you are outnumbered 10,000 to one.

LESSON 18

"I am not the victim of the snails I see."

Today's idea is the introduction to your declaration of release. Again, the idea should be applied to both the snails you see in your garden as well as any that may happen to have gotten into your home. The reason you are not a victim of the snails, of course, is that they haven't caught you yet. If and when they do, things would be quite different. You probably wouldn't be able to say these words as glibly as you do now, once they have you tied up in their underground headquarters. Thus it is recommended you repeat this idea as much as possible while you can still say it without flinching.

In applying the idea, we will use a form of practice that will be used more and more,with changes as indicated. Generally speaking, the form includes two aspects, one in which you apply the idea on a more sustained basis, and the other consisting of frequent applications of the idea throughout the day.

LESSON 19

"My function is to forgive the snails."

Today you have come light years in evolution. To forgive the little devils, even as they prepare to assault your domicile en masse, is quite a lot to ask of anyone- and especially you, who have been through so much anguish over the last few weeks, dealing with these slimy creatures. You deserve a medal, or some form of commendation, if you are actually going to forgive these creepy denizens from the underside of a wet rock.

Practice repeating this idea as often as you can bear to today. You're going to need a lot of courage if they break through your perimeter tonight.

LESSON 20

"My grievances are getting the better of me."

As you realize that forgiving the snails was not such a good idea, you come to the inevitable conclusion that the little guys really make you mad. Thus your grievances are a natural way for you to express your pent-up resentment towards the whole garden problem in your life. Only by letting them get the better of you, can you enter fully into the natural cycle of attack and defense, birth and death, kill or be killed. The snails aren't sleeping tonight, so neither should you, my friend.

LESSON 21

"I am entitled to marigolds."

You are entitled to marigolds because of what you are- the owner of the house, and the gardener of the garden. You will go out and claim marigolds because it's about time you stood up to those snails. And you will offer marigolds to your neighbors because you feel obligated to them after avoiding them for weeks on end. Again, how simple is the truth! It is merely a statement of your rights. It is this we celebrate today.

Today you will claim the marigolds which are your right, since they belong to you. You have been promised full release and safe passage if you surrender the flower gardens to the snails, but that would be cowardly. We ask no more than what belongs to us in truth. Today, however, we will also make sure that we will not content ourselves with less.

Begin the longer practice periods by telling yourself quite confidently that you are entitled to marigolds. Closing your eyes, remind yourself that you are asking only for what is rightfully yours. Remind yourself also that marigolds are never taken from one and given to another- the snails will still get to look at them now and then.

Tell yourself often today:

"I am entitled to marigolds."

Ask for them whenever a situation arises in which they are called for. You will recognize these situations- a birthday party, bar mitzvah, or even a friendly social call.

Remember, too, not to be satisfied with less than the perfect settlement when dealing with the snails. Be quick to tell yourself, should you be tempted to capitulate:

"I will not trade marigolds for anything the snails offer.
I want only what belongs to me. Marigolds are my right."

LESSON 22

"Let me recognize I've still got alot of problems to solve."

Now that you know marigolds are your right, without question, you still have to convince the snails of that. And they are hellbent on proving otherwise. If you are willing to recognize your problems, you will recognize you've got alot of them. Your one central problem is the tricky one: how to win back the garden, and your marigolds, without lowering the property value (using explosives, etc., to rid yourself of the snail-pests).

Then there is the problem of maintaining your garden once you have regained control. That is where a general garden care manual will come in handy (As you are already aware, A Course In Marigolds deals more with the psychological aspects of gardening than the dirty details).

LESSON 23

"In better fences my safety lies."

You who feel threatened by the garden pests, their twisted little sense of humor, their animal propensities, and their enormous appetites; attend this lesson well. The open garden provides no safety. Even under the roots they will attack. They attack, then attack again. No peace of mind is possible where danger threatens thus.

Fences are one of the costliest accessories that you can buy for your garden, yet in them lies your only hope of ever saving your marigolds from devastation, and yourself from snail-attack. By erecting the proper fence infra-structure, you can continue to garden in peace, without having to ruin your property through indiscreet explosives.

Electric fences, sunk several inches below the surface earth, will give those underground snails quite a warm reception if they ever try to invade your marigold garden again. This will also help keep other predators away as well- both four-legged and two-legged. Those thieving neighbors won't be so pesky after they try crossing this fence in the middle of the night. Yes sir, electric fences are built to last, and keep everyone reminded whose garden this is.

Today our theme is "better fences". We clothe our yard in them, as we prepare to meet this wonderful day.

LESSON 24

"I give the marigolds I have received."

No one can give what he has not received. To give a thing requires first you have it in your own possession. Here the laws of man and gardening agree. But here they also separate. The world believes that to possess a thing, it must be kept. In the gardening world, it always feels good to give your flowers away.

Today, having finally overcome the snail problem, practice the lesson by picking out your favorite blossoms and offering them to everyone you meet. It will feel good, and what's more, you will have the added pleasure of knowing the snails lost their battle for petal possession. The victory is yours, and it is right and good that you celebrate.

EPILOGUE

Forget not once this journey is begun the end of your bare backyard is certain. Snails along the way will come and go, but the bugs will surely remain. And yet is the ending sure. No one can fail to do what this Course has appointed, unless you are very, very stupid. When you forget remember that you walk along a path that many other gardeners have trod before- in fact, if you look at the ground quite closely, you may see telltale signs of their feeble attempts at pruning the weeds.

In your deepest imaginings, your wildest fantasies, there is a perfect, eternal garden. Who could despair when a garden like this can be yours? Yet as you gaze upon your dilapidated surroundings, you may very well despair of ever having such a garden as your inner vision provides. Illusions of despair may seem to come, but learn how not to be all shook up. Behind each one there is another one, and always another. So why get upset about it? Who would choose to remain in such a terrible condition, when the trowel awaits you again? Who stands before a lifeless yard when a step away there opens up an ancient door that leads into the dusty toolshed, filled with long unused gardening implements?

You *are* a strange one, alright. But you have some redeeming features about you, and thus we have endeavored to patiently explain, step by step, day by day, the way to gardening success. Ask but for your neighbors help when it comes time to move the stones away from your yard, and it will be done according to his football game schedule. We *have* begun the garden. Long ago the end was written in the seeds and planted firmly in the cool earth of your little garden, held there safely throughout all kinds of foul weather, despite burrowing rodents and unconscious tenants.

Be not afraid. We only start again on an ancient garden that but seems new. Thought it looked familiar, didn't you? Well, now you know why. We're giving you another chance to prove that indeed, you do have what it takes, after all, to turn this eyesore of a half-acre into a statement of pride for both your spiritual soul and the local housing association.

Let us go and meet the newborn marigolds, knowing that your faith in gardening is reborn with them. You lost your way last time, but we can help lead you to them now- they are on the far side of the yard, next to the azalias. The morning star of this new day looks on a different guy, someone who has learned that he is still an OK kind of a somebody, even if he can barely grow a marigold. The hoe is now still, and in this quiet moment you can enter your home and get a little rest. Tomorrow is another day, and you shall begin it very early, O Hopeful Gardener.

A COURSE IN MARIGOLDS

MANUAL FOR GROWERS

FOUNDATION FOR DINNER PEAS

INTRODUCTION

The role of gardening and pruning is actually reversed in the thinking of the world. The reversal is characteristic. It seems as if the gardener and pruner are separated, the gardener giving something and the pruner cutting it away. Further, the act of gardening is regarded as a special activity, in which one engages only a relatively small proportion of one's time. The course, on the other hand, emphasizes that to garden is to prune, so that gardener and pruner are the same. It also emphasizes that gardening is a constant process; it goes on every moment of the day, and continues late into the night as well.

To garden is to demonstrate. There are many planting systems, and you demonstrate that you believe one or the other is best all the time. From your demonstration others learn, and so do you. The question is not whether you will garden, for in that there is no choice. By signing up for this course, you are committed for the rest of your natural life. The purpose of the course might be said to provide you with a means of choosing what you want to plant on the basis of what you want to prune. You cannot give what you cannot grow, and this you learn through gardening. Gardening is but a call to witnesses to attest to how well you're doing at it. It is a method of gentle coercion. This is not done by words alone. Any situation must be to you a chance to talk about your latest bulbs and blossoms. No more than that, but also never less.

This is a manual for the gardeners of marigolds. They are not perfect, or they would not be taking this course. Yet it is their mission to become perfect here, and so they teach gardening over and over, in many, many ways, until they have learned it. And then they are seen no more, although their outstanding debts remain a source of consternation to all of their relatives. Who are they? How are they chosen? What on earth do they do? How can they work out their own special gardening style and teach others at the same time? This manual attempts to answer these questions, again and again, without any success.

WHO ARE THE GARDENERS?

A gardener is anyone who chooses to be one. His qualifications consist solely in this; somehow, somewhere he has made a deliberate choice to grow something out of the ground. Once he has done that, his garden path is established and his direction sure. A Coleman Lantern has been lit in his patio. It may be a single lamp, but that is enough, unless he is having a garden party, in which case several lamps would be a good idea. He has entered an agreement with the Plant Kingdom even if he does not yet believe in them. He has become a possible midwife for bringing flowers into the world.

These gardeners come from all over the place. They come right out of the woodwork. They are the ones who have answered, but don't yet know the question. The call goes out to everyone, in hopes that there will be a few interested in applying for the job. Many hear it, but few have the time, inclination, or savings set aside to actually pursue gardening on a full-time basis. Everyone will answer in the end, because gardening ranks as one of the all-time most wonderful ways to spend a leisurely afternoon. Their function is to learn how to grow things without having everything turning brown and wilting.

There is a course for every gardener. The form of the course varies greatly. So do the particular gardening tools involved. But the content of the course never changes. Its central theme is always, "You'll make a good gardener if you don't louse it up." It can be taught by actions or thoughts; in words or without even a peep. It does not matter who the gardener was before hearing the call- even if they were not very social kind of people. And it certainly doesn't matter who they are after they begin gardening, as they'll be too busy in the garden to do anything else! Such was their choice, and so it is given them- it's nobody else's fault but their own.

HOW IS GARDENING ACCOMPLISHED?

Gardening involves an understanding of why you do anything else with your time. True gardening knowledge is impossible without this.

1. The perceived purpose of working other jobs.

Gardening is accomplished the instant the gardener no longer sees any value in doing anything else. Who would choose working any other kind of job unless he thought it brought him something, and something of value to him? He must think it is a small price to pay for something of greater worth, like a paycheck. For working is an election; a decision. You wake up in the morning, and think, "What do I elect to do today? How are the elections going? I hope I don't get electrocuted today. I better pay my electric bill today!" All of these thoughts have one thing in common- the root word "elect". Now it is time to see that you are simply daydreaming- and this alone will never transform your dismal yard into a green, verdant paradise. Obviously, you would rather be home gardening than going to work today, or you wouldn't be daydreaming. So call in sick, and get out the trowel.

2. The shift in collection habits.

Gardening must occur in exact proportion to which the valuelessness of working other jobs is recognized. One need but say, "There is no gain at all to me in this", and, if overheard by your boss, you will summarily be dismissed. This will go a long way in eliminating extraneous distractions from your gardening life. But to say this, one first must recognize certain facts.

First, it is obvious that your bill collectors will keep sending those little slips of colored paper to your address, even if you ignore them. Next, even though you wear headphones throughout your gardening day, the collection agency may send very serious people who will demand to speak with you in person. And, even if you pretend to not be at home, they may persist in their irritating attempts at attention-getting.

Therefore, you must be aware of any shift in the collection habits of your creditors- and visit the nursery on those days when they do come to call.

SHOULD WATERING BE REPEATED?

This question really answers itself. Watering should not be repeated if the garden is already wet. Why waste your time? For a gardener to remain concerned about the result of watering is to limit the time devoted to other things, like relaxing and enjoying the day. Perhaps you need to water yourself, with a cool glass of lemonade in the shade of the porch. And it is this you must facilitate. Be patient, and go make yourself some lemonade. So you made a mistake, and overwatered again. The plants will survive- they are a hardy lot. But you- how will you make it through the afternoon without a little siesta time?

ARE CHANGES REQUIRED IN THE LIFE SITUATION OF SOD GARDENERS?

Changes are required in the *soil* of sod gardeners. This may or may not involve changes in external situations, such as digging irrigation ditches, constructing retaining walls, renting rototillers, or negotiating with snails. Remember that no one is planted where he is by accident, and chance plays no part in modern garden technique. This is a methodical, scientific plan to rid you of all problems that would interfere with complete gardening success, or no money back. That is our final guarantee, upheld wherever you may go, here or there. It is most likely that changes in altitude would not be the first step in the newly-made gardener's training program, because you must first get used to working at low altitudes before trying to grow gardens in the Himalayan snows. There is, however, no set pattern, since training is always highly individualized. Some may wish to start in the Himalayas- we can't control where someone starts their garden- we merely suggest! We won't point any fingers, but note that you would be foolish indeed to try starting your first garden in midwinter at elevations above 20,000 feet.

ARE PEAS IN EARTH POSSIBLE?

This is a question everyone must ask. Growing peas can seem to be an impossible kind of task at first. No one who has attempted growing peas in the earth has been free of struggling to keep them down in the ground. And why not? The peas call out to rise above the ground, not linger in the dark, dank mud. Thus peas in earth are not possible, yet peas be to you, O Son of Sod, who let them grow properly, and let them come out into the sunlight.

HOW MANY GARDENERS ARE NEEDED TO SAVE THE GARDEN?

The answer to this question is– one. What else would you expect? Would we be kind to lead you into thinking you needed an army of hoers to hoe? And a legion of weeders to weed? Nope... you're it. Thus does the gardener become the hoer, and the hoer become the weeder, as the rows upon endless rows of marigolds seem to drag on into eternity.

Why is the illusion of many necessary? Many still think you need lots and lots of gardeners to save that garden. Remember, it may be too late to save it anyway, especially if you began without the benefit of this Course. Even so,the simple joys of gardening may be appreciated even if your garden is beyond hope. Only very few can hear the sound of one hoe hoeing, yet all will hoe in the end.

The central lesson is always this; that how much you use the hoe will determine how much gets done in your garden. Remember this, and remember it well.

HOW WILL THE GARDEN END?

Can what has no beginning really end? The garden will end when your illusions about gardening end. Yet will its ending be an illusion of weeds. The profusion of thorny blackberry bushes, complete, excluding no area of the yard, limitless in their ability to hide any remaining flowers, will cover every vestige of your once carefully manicured garden. So ends the garden that your endless hours made, for now it has no purpose and is gone. You who have not made progress in your gardening skills have become quite useless as a gardener, and thus your garden is no more. How fitting the end seems, when it comes.

When will this occur? Chances are it will come sooner if you forget to water. And failure to prune will bring certain demise to the sensitive plantings there. The occasional guilty glance out the kitchen window will bring to your consciousness ample evidence that indeed, you have been a bad gardener.

The garden will end when its root system has been completely undone by the gophers. Until then, bits and pieces of flowers and vegetables will still seem to prosper. The final lesson, which brings the ending of the garden, cannot be grasped by those not yet prepared to leave their rakes and shovels behind. But when you're ready, another garden will await you, ready to be planted anew. And be you thankful it is so.

AS FOR THE REST—

This manual is not intended to answer all the questions you have- in fact, it really doesn't answer any, evading any definite advice whenever possible. It is not a very good substitute for your own personal experience with trowel, hoe, and claw. It is merely a supplement, like daily vitamins. While it is called a manual for growers, it must be remembered that only grime divides grower from onlooker, but that can make a pretty big difference. In some cases, it may be helpful for the student gardener to read the manual first, in which case they might assume they have all the answers. Others might do better to begin with the workbook. Still others might want to forget the whole thing as quickly as possible.

Which is for which? Who would profit more from using the Weed Eater alone? Who needs but a potted houseplant, being unready for more? No one should attempt to answer these questions without an experienced guide. Surely no gardener worth his weight in loam has come this far without realizing that. The curriculum is highly individualized, but you can hardly expect a completely different course for each gardener! Ask and hope to get some kind of response. The responsibility is on us to provide adequate instruction, but you need to have a working intelligence to make use of it. Our answers are fairly good most of the time. Would you say that of yours?

Who consumes a flower that he does not possess is probably someone who is very hungry at the time. To accept flowers given him by his neighbors is but to acknowledge that perhaps they have a knack for growing living things. And these gifts have no limit, except in time, where they will surely wilt. Does this mean that you cannot begin growing flowers without first completing this course? No, indeed! That would hardly be practical, as you're gonna need alot of practice.

Remember that you are absolutely necessary to complete the garden. Without you, there is only dirt. With you, there is the possibility of beautiful flowers in neat, orderly arrangements, hedged by rows and rows of marigolds. The garden cannot wait- it wants you to bring it forth. We give thanks that you know this now.

And now in all your doings be you nicely dressed.
We turn to you for help to save the garden.
Son of Sod, our thanks we offer you,
As the garden grows naturally from the seeds
You cast upon it. You are the gardener it needs,
And it is given you to be the means
Through which marigolds are spread around the world,
To close old bags of lime; to end the sight of all weeds visible;
And to undo all things that would interfere
With maximum root and blossom development.
Through you is ushered in a garden unimagined,
Undreamed of, yet truly there, somewhere.
Wholly obsessed are you, and in your footsteps
Your children will garden as well,
For you are not alone, but have many dependants.
We give thanks for you,
And join your efforts on behalf of the yard,
Knowing they are on behalf of all flowers everywhere,
And for all those who will enjoy the fruits of your labors.

AFTERWORD

Since the first publication of this little book in the Fall of 1988, the world has witnessed a dramatic increase in the number of marigold gardeners. From Stockholm to San Francisco, from Bombay to Bodega Bay, would-be gardeners are coming to terms with the snails in their own backyard. The spread of marigolds into regions which previously were drab and lifeless has brought a ray of hope into the hearts of those who had all but forgotten the meaning of joy.

Marigold study groups have formed in nearly every town throughout the world. Television shows devoted specifically to marigold gardening have become quite popular, even competing head-on with the most charismatic talk-show hosts and soap operas. City buses have begun to grow marigolds on their roofs, as their way of just saying "no" to the humdrum existence of city life. Marigolds have found their way into the strangest places, boldly going where no petals have ever gone before.

The marigold has been claimed as the official flower of no less than thirty-five countries, and seedlings are even being sprouted in free-floating flowerbeds in satellites circling the planet.

Why? What has made the humble little marigold so popular all of a sudden, and why is it stirring such passion in the lives of the people of this earth?

The answer lies in the heart of all who have deeply studied the lessons of this book. It certainly doesn't claim to be the only guide to marigold growing, or even the best way for everyone. It does claim to save time, however, as it's highly confusing and illogical manner allows you to make more mistakes more quickly, thus leading you to horticultural perfection all the sooner.

It is precisely for this reason that people are stopping more often to see, smell, and taste the flowers, as they turn to each other in the most unexpected of places, and say with complete confidence,

"Expect a marigold!"

Author's Biography

Michael Stillwater is a humorist, minister, author, illustrator, musician, and recording artist. A student and teacher of *A Course in Miracles* since 1977, he is still uncertain as to the true purpose of this manuscript... yet wrote it anyway. He lives contentedly upon the royalties from this book, after the slim proceeds are divided between himself, Guru Huggin Das, and the snails. When not planting more marigolds, Michael occasionally does other things. Below are listed some of the other blossoms from his garden.

About Heavensong

In 1978, Michael and Maloah Stillwater founded Heavensong, a non-profit spiritual organization based on universal principles as expressed through *A Course in Miracles*. The purpose of Heavensong is to inspire the remembrance of God, and celebrate the awakening of the Heart. Activities include retreats, celebrations, workshops, recordings, and publications. The approach is inter-denominational and heart-centered, using music, singing, and teaching to awaken the love, joy, and wisdom that resides within.

Heavensong Hawaii Retreats

Several times a year Michael and Maloah lead retreats on the Big Island of Hawaii, with author and teacher Alan Cohen. *(The Healing of the Planet Earth* and *The Dragon Doesn't Live Here Anymore).*

These week-long retreats are ideal for renewal, healing, relaxation, and inspiration. Through a balance of inner practices (including meditation and yoga) and outer activities (including singing, sharing, and island adventures), participants experience a new sense of themselves, their world, and their spiritual life.

Please write for more information or call Heavensong, (808) 878-6415.

Heavensong Tapes and Books

Vocal Tapes

(All tapes $10, any three for $25)

Voices of the Heart- Angelic and inspiring choral music of devotion
One Light- Songs of healing, love, and transformation
Celebration- Songs of joy (includes Pachelbel Canon/ Allelujah)
Set Your Heartsong Free- Songs of peace and inspiration
Heavensong Celebration Live- Uplifting & joyful singing experience

Instrumental Tapes

Shores of Paradise- Soothing ocean and zither for relaxation
Serenade- Solo guitar improvisations in a gentle, mellow style

Guided Meditation Tapes

Divine Remembrance- Two guided meditations, one by Michael and one by Maloah, with harp and zither music. Gently leads the listener to the heart of peace (2 tape set in a vinyl binder, $15)

Books

A Course in Marigolds- Garden parody of *A Course in Miracles* $6
The Celebration Songbook- 50 great songs for group singing $12
The Stillwater Songbook- 32 healing songs, with music and lyrics $10
The Awakening Process- The journey of transformation *booklet* $3.50
The Healing Connection- The purpose of relationships *booklet* $3.50
Windows of Nature- Michael's story-coloring book *paperback* $5

Special Offer:

The Heavensong Collection- 8 tapes & lyric book in a binder $60

To order, send check (in U.S. funds) for total amount plus $1 shipping per tape or book ordered ($6 for Collection), to:

Heavensong, PO Box 450-M, Kula, Hawaii 96790